Grassroots
A Step Dad's Que
Silverware
By Lee (Batesy) Bates.

To my partner Steph and step son Liam. Steph you give me strength every day to do what I do, you inspire me to be a better man, coach and HGV driver. Liam you are my world, you're bright, funny, kind hearted and everything I do in this world is for you. Also cheers to my two biological kids.

To the Midland Junior League committee, you are nothing but a bunch of rats.

Introduction

First of all thank you for buying
this coaching resource and

memoir. I believe that we should always be striving to develop as coaches and as people. I personally read about one book a year, last year it was "Pride and Prejudice". The year before that it was "Deano" the autobiography of Dean Windass. Both have heavily informed my practice as a coach. In this manual / memoir I will take you on a journey behind the scenes so you can see what it's like to work at the very bottom level. In this book I will outline what I think are the characteristics of a top grassroots football coach. They're things you won't hear on any sanctioned FA coaching course, these are real world tips that I've learned by spending years on the touchline, training pitch, in league meetings and disciplinaries. Inside these hallowed pages are everything you need to take your junior team from bottom of the table virgins to league winners.

Although not on the official reading list, this book can be used in conjunction to or instead of the UEFA A Licence.

Chapter 1: Setting Out Your Stall

"Success is not how high you have climbed, but how you

make a positive difference to the world." - Alan Pardew

When I first took over Boldmere Colts Under 8s in December 2018 they were a struggling team more concerned with participation and enjoyment than winning football matches. Before I took the reins the team were being "managed" by Gary Trew, one of the player's Dads. It was obvious to me that Gary had no clue how to organise a side, I watched on from in front of the respect barrier as he made pointless substitution after pointless substitution, giving everyone a turn and never really getting a foothold in the game. Don't get me wrong Gary Trew was a nice bloke, worked hard in his IT day job, probably a good Dad but it was clear to me from the way he managed in his pack-a-mac and Asics running trainers that the man was a born loser. At half-time with the team 3-0 down he spoke about "playing with a smile on their faces" advice which one kid Kian took literally, playing the entire second half with a deranged grin etched across his face whilst the opposition passed the ball around him effortlessly. As the final whistle blew I was already sitting in my car thinking "maybe I've bitten off more than I can chew this time."

2 Weeks Earlier

I'd not long moved in with Steph and her son Liam after the break-up of my first marriage. I met Steph in the Sutton Coldfield Branch of Dixon's, I was taking back a faulty Beko Microwave which they were refusing to give me a refund on as I;

"hadn't purchased it from this or any Dixon's store." They were right, I'd gotten it for nothing off my mate Pelsy, I was moving into a flat near the town centre and needed to do it on the cheap. The first day I had it I was warming through a tuna pasta bake when it started smoking, I rang Pelsy but he wasn't answering his phone. Anyway I explained all this to the lad behind the till and he was having none of it. As I turned to walk out the store and maybe put my foot through a washing machine door on the way, there she was. Stood in the queue looking resplendent, holding a cream Russell Hobbs Toaster. I was instantly taken aback and it took every ounce of courage inside me to go and introduce myself. She had this look in her eye that I'll never forget, it was like magic I was drawn to her and I could tell from the way her voice crackled that she was drawn to me, either that or she had some sort of underlying respiratory problems. We chatted for a moment and I could feel some chemistry between us. At that moment our gaze was broken by a crashing sound coming from over by the entertainment section. A young boy about 6 had used a group of wall mounted plasma TVs as a climbing frame. As he'd reached the summit he'd managed to pull off one of its brackets and was now lying on the floor crying. This was my first introduction to Liam. Although I did and still do technically have a biological son, from that moment there was a very unique bond between me and Liam. He's destructive in the way I am, he's a tortured soul, there is a fire in him and I knew then that if I could help him harness that fire he could go on to achieve great things. If I could get him to channel that anger and aggression into sport rather than towards electrical goods I could help him flourish.

Sitting in the car on that wet Saturday morning I had to make a decision, do I take on Boldmere Colts Under 8s, give up my weekends plus 5 nights a week for training and try to build something? Or do I carry on coasting, driving lorries at night through the week and then going out with the lads at the weekend. As Ocean Drive by the Lighthouse family funnelled through the speakers thoughts drifted to my childhood, playing youth football and the role my own father had taken. My Dad John, was a very hands on father, he helped out with all of the groups in the community, he was treasurer for my youth side, treasurer for the scout group and my sister's dance school. During the daytimes he worked hard in a factory which made car parts. Despite receiving incapacity benefit for a bad back he worked 40 hours a week on the production line. In the evenings he'd carry out his voluntary work looking after the books of the local community groups, taking subs, paying fees, nothing was too much trouble for treasurer John. Then one day in the Summer of 1992 my old man disappeared. In what was a massive coincidence all of the money from the football club, scouts and dance school had also gone missing. There were a lot of rumours at the time but my own theory is that he'd clocked off from work and was on the way to the bank to pay in club funds when he was involved in a bank heist in which he was kidnapped and all of the money stolen. There was a real spate of burglaries in the area at the time because when me and mum got home from the police station someone had broken in and stolen all of Dad's clothes out of the wardrobe. I thought about how my Dad had been wronged by the game, I thought of Liam at home, bored needing an outlet and I thought "Batesy lets fucking ave it." I got out of the car, marched over to Gary and said

"I'll take the job."

Initially he had no idea what I was talking about or who I was. I explained that I'd seen his post looking for help on the community Facebook page a week earlier. I had gone on there to publicly slam local Indian Restaurant Ikbal's Kitchen who took over an hour and a half to deliver a chicken Bhuna when I saw Gary's plea. I told Gary that I was keen and really think I could work wonders with this group of players so much so that I'd offer to work for free for 6 months. Gary explained that the role was entirely voluntary and after some thought I accepted and couldn't wait to get cracking. There was no time for a DBS check, these lads needed my help and fast. I knew that if I was going to make a success of this club I needed to put my own stamp on it.

I hit the ground running at Boldmere Colts Under 8s. The first thing I did before I even learnt the player's names was cancel the Christmas disco. There was a real party culture at the club. It seemed to be every week that it was someone's birthday or trip to a theme park. and I knew I had to stamp that out if we were going to start competing. In that very first game I watched from the sidelines on a freezing December morning it was clear to me that some of those kids were more concerned about seeing Santa than they were tracking back.

The next thing I did was to sign Liam onto the team, it was the outlet he needed. I also thought some added responsibility would help him so I immediately made him captain. This ruffled a few feathers amongst the parents as Liam was technically two years too old to sign for an under 8s side. I explained that the rules are there to be bent and our ethos as a club was now about winning games and anyone who didn't want to be part of that was out the door. Gary Trew was the first parent I clashed with; Gary kept talking about how this was a family team brought together by a group of parents to provide an opportunity for their kids to play football. It was that kind of participation mindset I had to rid from the club. With that in mind I signed a new goalkeeper Yuri. Again he was a few years older than the recommended age limit but Yuri was a refugee and luckily for us had no record of his birth date. He also had no idea where his parents were so I said that he could move in with Gary. There were some teething problems at first due to the language barrier but I would like to think that despite the eventual break-up of his marriage Gary would love back at this as a positive experience.

Chapter 2 Creating A Club Mentality

"The family is the test of freedom, because the family is the only thing the free man makes by himself and for himself." - Steve Bruce

It wasn't just on the pitch that I needed to make changes. For too long Boldmere Colts had been a social club for parents'. I'd turn up at training and I'd hear them catching up on life and planning social gatherings. I had to stop that as soon as possible. I needed everyone to muck in if I was going to make this thing a success. If I was doing my bit on the pitch, working with the players, sorting tactics etc I need them to help me off the pitch. First of all we needed sponsorship. A good sponsor can help buy those more expensive club items that no team can do without; like match day kit, rain jackets and interactive whiteboards. Our current sponsors were the local taxi firm who I thought would be too small-fry to support what we were trying to achieve. 3 ford Mondeos and a 7 seater for airport jobs was not a business that was going to sustain our long term ambitions. I instructed one of the mum's Tara who works in PR to contact some of the biggest businesses in the country. As someone who believes in leading by example I did the same and on one Tuesday afternoon spent 6 hours on the phone to Virgin trying to secure a deal, their advisor Tariq seemed more concerned about selling me a TV bundle than he did discussing the genuine business proposition I had called about. In the end Tara managed to secure us a sponsorship deal with "Planet of the Vapes", a local vape shop in town. As part of the deal they would not only give us money for kit but also provide refillable vape juice for all players over the age of 12. With this cash in my back pocket I went out and ordered a new kit, bright white like the Galecticos of Real Madrid, I also got myself a brand new tracksuit with my initials and on it and a polo shirt for Gary who I'd decided to keep on as my assistant for a bit of continuity (for the time being at least). Branding is important for any successful organisation and I saw no reason why junior football should be any different. For this reason I decided that it would be all hands on deck to modernise the club facilities. When I first got there the only "facility" available was an old porta-cabin left behind by some builders over 6 years ago. I instructed all parents and wider family members to get involved in decorating the porta cabin in true DIY SOS style, whilst I oversaw the whole thing in sort of a Nick Knowles capacity. I often think about just how badly Nick Knowles would be bullied on an actual building site. Not discernible practical skills, straight out of drama school, doesn't bear thinking about. With two weeks of hard graft from all of the parents and with the help of some local tradesmen I'd pretty much begged to give up their time to help us free of charge, the tired old porta-cabin was fit for purpose. We had proper laminate flooring put down, a hot water urn for teas and coffees and even a chemical toilet (not for solids). I even got the owner of the vape shop to come and cut the ribbon in front of the local press. When all the work was completed I took a step back and looked upon what we'd achieved as a collective and I felt a real sense of pride. I also felt that this wasn't enough and decided to move the team to a completely different site which already had changing rooms on hand. Sometimes you have to dream big to achieve big.

Every top manager needs a loyal assistant and it became apparent pretty early doors that Gary Trew was just not going to cut it. Gary's son Willow (I know) played for the team and although Gary's heart was in the right place he just wasn't an elite level operator. A perfect example of this was when Gary signed up for the 2019 London Marathon to raise money for Guide Dogs UK. I initially of course was supportive as Guide Dogs UK is a great charity; for too long our money has been sent to overseas guide dogs and I was delighted to see some of that money staying in Britain. Gary wasn't a natural runner but trained hard leading up to the race and eventually managed to stumble round in just over 6 hours. Now to me I'd rather not finish than fail to break the 5 hour mark, when people have put their hands in their pockets and left messages on your JustGiving page clock that kind of time is nothing short of disrespectful in my opinion, sprained ankle or not. Gary just wasn't a football man, if you were to ask him who his favourite player was he'd say David Seaman because of his performances on Dancing on Ice and whilst David was surprisingly nimble out on the ice for a big man, that lack of football knowledge simply wouldn't do. Within two months of being at Boldmere I made the unprecedented call to manage the team alone without an assistant. I'd keep Gary on to help with logistics and setting up on match days, putting out bibs and cones, collecting subs, taking training when I was away, organising referees, taking minutes at parents meetings, attending first aid courses but I would be a lone ranger. A one man management team.

Although there were some initial teething problems off the pitch, things on the pitch couldn't have been going much better. With Yuri almost unbeatable in goal and a kick that could clear the whole pitch we became really hard to beat. I had to drop some dead wood of course, releasing one player who had been with the team since the age of 4, this was a tough call and not an easy text to send. But the lads who remained were enjoying it, we were playing well every week one highlight being a mauling of local rivals Gilway in a cup fixture. Gilway were down a man and so in the spirit of sportsmanship I lent them one of our players. I thought that was the noble thing to do but when young Kian notched 3 own goals the opposition royally kicked off. So much so that things became heated afterwards and I had no choice but to report them for fielding an ineligible player. There was a lot of that in the early days, we ruffled a lot of feathers in the local junior league. Little old Boldmere Colts who were the league's whipping boys had turned things around and other teams in the area simply did not like it. Once during a home game against St Thomas's a local catholic side, their manager Father Michael O'Leary accused one of our parents of poor sportsmanship. Unfortunately for the Vicar he picked on the wrong parent. Ethan's Dad Mick was an ex football hooligan who had done time in prison following an incident in Marbella in the early 1990s. Mick had reportedly smashed up a bar on the seafront and when local police arrived he was in such a rage that they tear-gassed him. Wild with anger and blind from the tear gas he began choking a female diner on the next table and was sentenced to six months in a Spanish prison. The worst part of the whole thing was that there wasn't even a game on at the time, Mick was on a family holiday when this all happened.

But I embraced all the characters we had around the club at the time, I think you have to. One set of parents Stu and Indi were what I like to call "modern parents". They didn't believe in discipline in the traditional sense, they let their son River (don't get me started) make his own rules. If he chooses to go to school great, if he chooses to eat Smarties for dinner, fine, it's his choice. I can't say it's a parenting style I agree with. Once young River was on the bench, I tried to bring him on in defence but he refused claiming that he "identified" as a striker, I'd never heard anything like it in my life. I went ballistic and booted his wheatgrass smoothie across the touchline, Stu and Indi were far from impressed and I no doubt came in for some criticism on the weekly podcast which they record. There are always teething problems but with Boldmere Colts sat pretty second in the league with a game in hand, people were starting to buy into Batesy's way of doing things.

Chapter 3 - Overcoming Barriers

"Always bear in mind that your own resolution to success is more important than any other one thing." - Bradley Walsh (Soccer Aid)

I always say to my players at training, that in life, it's never a straight line to the things you want, they usually respond with something like,

"But you said we would have a game at the end."

But my point is that no matter what you are trying to achieve there are always people out there who will put stumbling blocks in your way and in March 2019 I was presented with an almighty one. I was conducting a strength and conditioning session with the under 8s when I was approached by a lady in a navy trouser suit. I initially thought it was a rep from CO-OP travel doing some outreach sales work but when she introduced herself as Sheila the club's Welfare Officer my heart sank. Until this point I genuinely had no idea that Boldmere Colts had a Welfare Officer, I believed we were a stand alone outfit out there on our own against the world. Sheila explained that Boldmere Colts are actually one of the largest junior clubs in the region with at least two teams at every age group and that I would know all about this if I had turned up at the "club meetings" she'd "continuously "invited" me to. This was news to me, I vaguely recall an email from Gary with an agenda one time but I assumed his ex-wife had hacked his account again. I had no idea about these club meetings at all. I of course was holding parent's meetings every fortnight to discuss any issues arising. In fact just a week earlier we sat round as a group as I proposed introducing a series of team fines for lateness, loss of kit and foul throw-ins. Then Sheila uttered two words that to this day send shivers down my spine; "Charter Standard". Sheila explained that for Boldmere to maintain its Charter Standard status all of it's coaches must have an FA Level 1 coaching certificate. I of course didn't possess such a qualification. I explained that I didn't see the need to formalise my knowledge, I've been around the game for years and there's nothing that an FA pen pusher with a clipboard could teach me about the beautiful game. But I explained that I was open to compromise and if the club were willing to pay I would consider doing my UEFA Pro licence which would allow me to manage professionally on the continent. Sheila stated that the FA level 1 was compulsory and that she'd already booked me on for the following weekend.

I'll be honest I turned up on the first weekend of my level 1 with an air of cynicism. I'd checked into a nearby hotel the night before and spent the night re-watching the Pep Gulardiola documentary on the tablet that Liam had gotten me for father's day. Where the course was being held was actually only about 4 miles from my house but

I thought if I'm going to do this then I want the full experience. I thought I'd go to the course in the day time and then unwind over a few drinks with the rest of my candidates in the evening. As it happened the rest of the people on the course also lived pretty locally so I was the only one staying over but I was determined to make the best of it. On the first morning of the course we all had to go around the room and introduce ourselves. There were people there from all different backgrounds, there were mum's and dad's just trying to understand more about how to help their kids play football. There were a few college kids trying to get a qualification under their belts. But there was one guy in that room who stood out instantly for me. Jim Bentom addressed the group with an authority which said "I've been around the block a few times." Jim had been managing in the lower leagues for years but when his first son was born he signed up to do his coaching badges before his wife was even discharged from hospital. Jim was a real character, he was an ex-pro at Brentford although there is no formal record of this due to a clerical error which Jim is still disputing through the courts. I'll never forget one afternoon on the course, one of the other candidates was leading a session on shooting and picked Jim out to do a demonstration. In goal at the time was another candidate; June, a retired PE teacher in her late 60s. Part of the practice included Jim going through on goal one-on-one vs June. Jim took an uncharacteristically heavy touch out of his feet and when June came out to claim the loose ball Jim, who was easily 16 stone slid two-footed into June taking her and ball into net. June became entangled in the netting like a panicked carp and eventually had to be cut free by the course tutor. We didn't see June again after that but that was Jim, he wore his heart on his sleeve and that's why I liked him so much. Me and Jim had a riot on that course, we'd cause havoc for the other candidates, one young lad Ryan had to do a session on short passing and I deliberately miss-placed every pass in the 15 minute practice. Jim will tell you that I wasn't doing it on purpose and it was in fact just a lack of ability but that's the kind of joker he was. By the end of the course I think the poor tutor was glad to see the back of us but I think deep down he knew me and Jim were destined for big things in the management game even saying;

"You two have no place in junior football."

This was him telling me to move into the professional men's game but I was loyal to Boldmere and I couldn't wait to implement what I'd learned out there on the training pitch. On the day of my final assessment Boldmere had a crucial league game against a team just outside the top 4. I unfortunately couldn't be there as I was on the course so Gary had to take charge of the team. To be honest this worried me. Gary hadn't been the same since his wife left and he was struggling to bring up Yuri as a single parent. I phoned Gary at full time and asked how they'd gotten on, he uttered the words that I had dreaded;

"The kids really enjoyed it."

They'd been beaten, I knew it. This would leave us 6 points off top spot without a game in hand. I'll be honest I wanted to quit there and then. But I knew in my heart I had to see this through. That afternoon I had to be a "body" in more of the candidate's sessions. I played like a man possessed all afternoon, foxes and rabbits, king of the ring, over and under, cones and dishes, I poured my heart out into every session. So much so that by the time it came for my own assessment I was too exhausted to stand, I lay on the astro-turf cramping up, barking out orders at the other candidates. I'd done it, I'd scraped through by the skin of my teeth, I'd done what only 99.9% of FA level 1 candidates managed to do, I'd passed. I was chuffed and invited Steff and Liam plus a few family members to the graduation which was actually just the course tutor handing me a certificate in a one to one meeting. Quite the anti-climax after two weekends of hard graft but nevertheless I was delighted and couldn't wait to put the things I'd learnt into practice. I also knew I'd made a friend for life in Jim Benton. Unfortunately I haven't actually heard from Jim since graduation but if I know Jim he'll be on a touchline somewhere giving people what for.

Chapter 4 Staying Power

"Life's not about how hard you can hit, it's about how hard you can get hit and keep moving forward." - Tony Pulis

With my FA level one under my belt and an emergency aid qualification resit pending. I just wanted to crack on with managing the team, but the universe presented me with yet more hurdles. On the pitch things were going great guns; Liam in particular was having a real purple patch winning "player of the week" for 8 weeks on the bounce. Some parents said this was favouritism especially as he hadn't even played in two of the games during that period. Liam was really enjoying his football and we'd become closer than ever as step dad and step son. We would watch TV together, go on long walks with the dog and I'd even play on his video games with him. I'd also play them without him, all day whilst he was at school, I actually developed a slight addiction to Fortnight at one point. Things between Steph and I though had taken quite a nosedive. It was during this time Steph felt that I was neglecting her, that I was too focussed on the team and that we weren't spending enough time together as a couple. Things came to a head one evening when I took her out for a pub meal to make amends. I swear to this day that I had no idea that there was a league meeting scheduled in that pub for the exact time and day that we were in there. Steph didn't believe me though and stormed out. I would have gone after her but there were some key points being raised around player registrations which I could ill afford to miss. Steph can be fiery. I knew that from the start, I think it's where Liam gets it from but this felt different. Steph told me to move out of the family home for a while whilst I, as she put it "got my priorities" right. This was a difficult time, I moved myself in with Gary and Yuri, Gary insisted that there wasn't room but I explained that if he moved his model train set into the shed then he could easily fit a queen sized bed into the spare room. I began to spiral downhill over the next 7 days, I wasn't washing properly, I wasn't eating, I was just staying in my room all day masturbating. One evening I was tugging myself raw when there was a knock at my door. It was Yuri;

"Coach" he said in his thick european accent.

"Do not come in Yuri." I pleaded as I desperately tried to cover up my throbbing member.

I put some trousers on and opened my bedroom door. Yuri stood there on the landing with a tear in his eye holding an old black and white photograph of what I assumed was his family. Yuri began to open up to me, explaining that he had no idea where his family were or if he'd ever see them again. He told me that they were forced to flee their home due to extreme poverty but somehow he'd become separated from them and had no way of tracking them down. There we were, two broken men pulled apart from our families. At this moment Gary joined us on the landing and started to speak about how much he missed his wife but by this point the time for wallowing was over. I stopped Gary dead in his tracks and as we stood there, three broken men on a landing I knew I had to do what I was born to do. Lead, I said, I "Listen lads, we might me down but we are most definitely not out, tomorrow is a new day, tomorrow we get up, we get out there and we get back what is rightfully ours."

Then I went back into Gary's spare room and masturbated like I'd never masturbated before.

You see I'd been treating Steph like a reserve team player, giving her very little attention whilst I focussed on the first team lads. This can work in the short term but over a long period those reserve team players start to become resentful and so you have to throw them on for 20 minutes in a cup game here and there to keep them happy. It was time for me to show Steph just how much she meant to me. I picked her up the following morning, putl a blindfold on her and drove her to where it all began.

As we pulled up to the Sutton Coldfield branch of Dixons it suddenly dawned on me that it had closed down 6 months earlier and was now a Carpet Right. Steph who had become very impatient by this point ripped the blindfold off and said; "Why the fuck have you brought me to a carpet shop?"

I had to think on my feet. I looked her in the eyes as I spoke.

"Our love is like a carpet, it is at the base of our home, it's warm and durable, it provides continuity, sure it might get stained from time to time but with the right chemicals…"

I was losing her at this point.

"Many many others, have trodden on it but ours comes

with a ten year garuntee and I'll
be damned if I'm just going to rip
that thing up and put down some
laminate."
This had become nonsensical
by this point but Steph just
looked at me like she always did
and smiled, then I smiled and
then we kissed. We made up,
we always made up. That was
us, we were meant to be
together, I agreed to stop
constantly thinking about football
and to start putting her first. I
even managed to convince her
to put the blindfold back on so I
could sneakily run into the
sports shop next to Carpet Right
and grab a pack of Sondico
bibs.

I made big changes after this, I started putting family first, I dropped training down to 4 nights a week, I left all of the team whatsapp groups. Some parents would say that I was actually removed because of a video I sent in by accident but I was making a conscious effort to do right by my family. I even made the effort to track down my own son Callum. I managed to find his number which I had saved in my phone. Callum told me that he'd moved to France on a Rugby scholarship, it of course wasn't what I would have chosen for him but I was proud nonetheless. We agreed to meet up when the season had finished. I also had to make changes on the pitch.

Unfortunately for everyone Yuri had to step back from the team as he'd taken on some full time warehouse work and whilst he was still living under Gary's roof rent free Saturday's were now a no go. I started giving fringe players more game time. Players who'd I'd written off as crap or not worthy were now being given a chance. Sure we weren't winning as many games but there was a real feeling of community around the team and amongst the parents. It really was something that money couldn't buy.

Chapter 5 - A Never Say Die Attitude

"Don't give up before the miracle happens." - Steve McClaren

As I look back on that time now I can see I was in a haze and if I hadn't have snapped out of it when I did Boldmere Colts under 8s would have been mid-table finishers in the 18/19 season. Fortunately for me, divine intervention came in the shape of Jim Benton.

With Boldmere sitting 5th in the League with 6 games to go I decided to go for a full English Breakfast at a cafe in town before our midday kick-off. I was thumbing through the paper when I heard a familiar voice bellowing from the back of the cafe.

"You can share a lemonade between you, I'm not fucking made of money."

It was Jim Benton. Ever the family man, Jim was out with his two kids for a bite to eat. I immediately went over with the intention of catching up on old times. Now here's the strange thing. Jim clearly had no recollection of who I was, not a clue, he looked straight through me like I was a sheet of glass. It was clear to me that one of two things was happening here. Either it wasn't Jim; I'd been guilty in the past of recognising people incorrectly. I once approached a man who I was convinced was Sir Elton John at Keele services. Unfortunatley it turned out to just be another gay fella in sunglasses. I did wonder at the time why Elton was driving a Honda Civic but I'd always been a big fan of his work so went over and said hello. But I was 100% certain this was Jim, we'd had such a good laugh on the level one course that I'd know that smile anywhere and I knew there was no way he would've forgotten me. The other more upsetting possibility here was that Jim had suffered some kind of brain injury completely wiping out his mid to long term memory. This was heartbreaking, to see a man of that stature reduced to just a shell of the man, not even able to remember his closest friends almost brought me to my knees. Amazingly Jim was still driving and as I watched him speed off before his kids had even got his seatbelts on I was struck with a sense of just how fleeting life was. I had an overwhelming feeling, a feeling that I wanted to be remembered, not just by Jim but by the world.

As I turned up at the match later that day the old Lee Bates was back, it was no more Mr Nice Guy. During the warm up one of the kids blazed the ball over the bar and I barked at him.

"You miss the target you fetch your own shit,"

This is something I stand by, players need to learn that if you miss the target you have to fetch your own ball. Unbeknownst to me, the pitch that day backed onto the A38 and poor Sam was almost killed, but it's like I explained at the tribunal, players need to learn to get their head over the ball.

I'd joined this club to win the league and by god that's what I was going to do. That afternoon we went out and thumped a side that sat at the bottom of the league. Still parents weren't happy, we'd won 14-0 and I still had people moaning that their kid had had zero game time. I was learning that I was never going to please everyone. We went on and won the next 4 putting us 2nd in the league with two to play. Game on.

Chapter 6 - Man Management

"Innovation distinguishes
between a leader and a
follower." - Nigel Pearson

In my opinion man or for those
working at the lower levels of the
game women management is
one of the most important skills
for any coach to master. Each
player is different, some young
players might want a rocket
around their shoulder others
might need an arm up their arse.
It's vital to know which approach
to take when working with
players of any age. Some

players are simple, some are more complex and with 2 huge games coming up I needed everyone to be on top form. I made the bold call to throw a team building day and boost morale ahead of these crucial fixtures. We hired a 60 seater coach and invited players, parents and grandparents on board for a trip to Wembley for a stadium tour. I'd only been to Wembley once before and that was for Take That's 2009 Circus Tour. The lads were fantastic, 12 years out of the game had not taken their toll on Gary, Robbie, Mark and the other two, it really was an incredible show. That was special but every coach dreams of leading their team out at Wembley and that day I became one of the few managers to actually do it. Granted it was only a stadium tour but when I led the lads onto the pitch that day I was bursting with pride. We weren't actually allowed onto the pitch and I was heavily reprimanded for even setting foot on the grass but it was worth it to touch that hallowed turf.

To be honest I thought I'd get there as a player, I was a promising school boy with lots of potential. I was sought after by all of the local teams and mum would take me to train with a new team almost every week before deciding that club wasn't for me and moving me on. I did eventually settle down and sign for a local side Dalton. Dalton

FC were run by a local PE teacher Mr Wilks. Mr Wilks was a good soul and did his best by the lads. Unfortunately one day my mum received a call from Mr Wilks on the house phone to say that due to a lack of funding the team would have to fold, there'd be no more training, no matches, nothing. Later that day we were walking in the park when we saw Mr Wilks and the team training. God bless him, he hadn't had the heart to tell the rest of the lads that they were folding. I thought it best not to go over and break the news. It actually took Mr Wilks a further 4 years to let the lads know that they'd be stopping the team after just 3 more years of competitive games.

The kids loved Wembley, some of their favourite players had played there. At one point we went into the changing rooms. I went and sat in one of the booths and thought about all of the legends that have sat in that spot over the years, David Beckham, Wayne Rooney, Mark Owen. This really was a special day, all of the kids and parents were beaming and I was so glad that I was able to give them this experience for just £88pp (not including lunch or transport). A magical day.

Unfortunately things took a turn for the worse on the way home. We'd been on the road for about an hour when it suddenly dawned on me. Where was Kian? Kian Burrows was one of those kids who things just happened to. Most of his first season with the club was blighted by impetigo, his condition was so contagious that he wasn't allowed to train or play matches for about six months. During that time we did bring him back for one match against a team with one very talented player, Kian man marked him and the lad was reduced to scratching his own skin off by half time and had to be substituted. Kian was categorically one of the worst footballers I have ever worked with and people say that the only reason I kept him at the club was because I had a soft spot for his mum. I don't deny that Sally was a lovely woman with a fantastic range of sports leggings but there was another reason I kept Kian on board, morale. The kid was an absolute hoot. Once during an away game Kian had got so confused at one of Gary's team talks that he just burst into tears, it was absolutely hilarious. I got on the PA system on the coach and after a brief rundown of the day and a football based quiz I asked;

"Has anyone seen Kian?"

By this point we were back at the clubhouse and one the other kids Sam said that he'd last seen Kian picking up a pile of mugs which he'd knocked over in the gift shop. Kian's mum Sally, who hadn't joined us on the trip much to my disappointment, was beside herself. I did the only thing I could do and offered to drive me and Sally straight back down to Wembley to pick Kian up. Mick had phoned ahead to say that we were on our way. As we drove down the M1, Boys2Men on the stereo I thought of all the extra things I do for these players and how I was happy to do it, these kids meant the world to me. We got down as far as Milton Keynes when my phone rang. It was Stu explaining that he and Indi were away on a yoga retreat that weekend coming and he wondered if I could pick River up and take him to the game, I explained that I wasn't a babysitting service and that he'd have to get an uber or something. Stu launched into a rant about the ethics of Uber as a company and left me with no choice but to put the phone down.

Me and Sally arrived back in London about 9pm to find Kian there waiting with a burley security guard. Sally hugged them both and thanked the security guard for keeping her boy safe. He said it was the least he could do for such a lovely lady, urgh what a creep. I was starving by this point so suggested we all went for a Nando's and whilst we were in London anyway, why not grab a west end show? Sally wanted to get home so we hopped back in the car and headed back up north. As I drove home in the dead of night I looked in my rearview mirror, he was curled up asleep on the seats and I thought to myself, I better get those seats valletted, can't risk Liam catching one of his many skin conditions.

Chapter 7 - A Winning Mentality

"Champions aren't made in gyms. Champions are made from something they have deep inside them – a desire, a dream, a vision. They have to have last-minute stamina, they have to be a little faster, they have to have the skill and the will. But the will must be stronger than the skill. - Alan Curbishley

May 3rd 2019 the sun shone, the grass was lush, all subs were paid and Boldmere Colts Under 8s were ready for one of the most defining days in the clubs history. A top of the league showdown with arch rivals St Thomas's, winner takes all. This is what we'd worked towards all year and we knew that today was our time. St Thomas' superior goal difference meant that only a Boldmere victory would secure the title. I'd never seen so many parents at a match day, even the increased admission fee of £9 hadn't seemed to put people off. There were grandparents on deck chairs, younger brothers and sisters flying kites, Mick had even brought his own BBQ and was selling bacon and sausage cobs behind one of the goals. In fact this BBQ generated so much smoke that it impeded the opposition goalkeeper's view for a first goal, their parents were fuming but we'd take it. 1-0 Boldmere. Just after half-time a mistake by Kian led to their equaliser. An eczema flare up had meant that he was playing the whole game with E45 on his hands, when he took a throw-in deep inside his own half he lost grip of the ball and their striker pounced, putting it high into the roof of the net. 1-1. It was squeaky bum time. Both sides pressed for an equaliser but it was advantage St Thomas's due to their goal difference. With the clock ticking down the ball fell to Liam on the edge of the box. Liam, ever the team player, with the goal gaping passed the ball to Kian who was in a better position. Kian slipped to the ground and the ball bounced off his back. It appeared that the chance had gone but a lucky break meant that the ball was back at Liam's feet. This time he wasn't going to pass, Liam got his head over the ball just like I'd always told him and drilled it as hard as he could towards the goal. BANG. It again had hit Kian in the base of the spine sending him into spasm. Fortunately for us it had landed back at Liam's feet and this time he calmly tucked it away, 2-1 Boldmere. The players went wild, trampling all over Kian's fallen body as they celebrated, me and Gary punched the air in celebration. There was barely time for the opposition to kick off before the final whistle went. We'd done it. League champions. I dropped to my knees for a moment before lying down fully on my back in the centre circle and began to sob, this felt amazing. The kids celebrated, the parents celebrated. In the midst of the hysteria I had an overwhelming urge to phone my son Callum. "Callum, son, we won the league." I screamed into the phone.

"That's great Dad, we had our cup final today to…"

I'd already put the phone down. I was too excited. There were some concerns about Kian's wellbeing as he hadn't moved in the 3 minutes since the final whistle but I just knew he'd be over the moon once he found out he'd claimed his first ever assist. I was in tears as I gave the 15 year old referee his £9 payment. All that was left was for us to be presented with the league trophy. I know it was presumptuous but I'd asked my mate Pelsy the week earlier to erect a podium next to the small sided pitch for the presentation and he'd done a brilliant job; it looked like something worthy of the Champions League final.

"Is there someone from the league here to present the trophy to us? Or is there a special guest that does it?" I asked the ref.

"No there is no trophy?" the young referee answered timidly.

"What?"

"Under 8s play non-competitive football, there are technically no official league rankings and there certainly isn't a trophy."

I was gutted, what had all this been for if there wasn't even a trophy at the end of it? I guessed it was pointless even asking about prize money and so I just walked off in disgust. I felt empty, a year's worth of work, for nothing. I stood in the centre circle and looked around for a moment. I saw laughter and happiness. I saw parents bonding with their children, I saw kids playing with each other, giggling, kicking a ball around, you know just being kids. Just then Steph and Liam came bounding over and hugged me. "Thanks for everything Dad." Wow. My heart stopped, He'd just called me Dad. Steph squeezed me tightly and for about a minute I was lost in pure nirvana, my life felt complete. This was it. This is was the greatest prize. I thought maybe ther real silverware is famil…. "Batesy?" Mick called out as he came storming across the pitch. "I've just got off the phone and guess what? I've ordered us a big fuck off trophy." GET IN!

Epilogue

Thank you so much for reading. I hope you enjoyed this short book. Lee Bates "Grassroots Coach" is the creation of stand-up comedian Josh Pugh. This book was written during the closure of all live events and public gatherings due to the 2020 Coronovairus. By buying this book and sharing it with others you are supporting the arts during this uncertain time. Thanks again and please continue to follow @GrassrootsCoac5

Cheers

Josh x

@JoshPughComic

Other books to come in the series:

Grassroots - A decade of dominance.

Grassroots - Keeping Your Nose Clean (Women's football special)

Grassroots - The Academy Years

Printed in Great Britain
by Amazon

79071509R00046